OH, THAT'S
RIDICULOUS!

Also by William Cole
and Tomi Ungerer

OH, WHAT NONSENSE!
OH, HOW SILLY!

OH, THAT'S
RI*DIC*ULOUS!

POEMS SELECTED BY WILLIAM COLE

DRAWINGS BY TOMI UNGERER

THE VIKING PRESS   NEW YORK

FIRST EDITION

Text copyright © 1972 by William Cole. Illustrations copyright © 1972 by Tomi Ungerer. All rights reserved. First published in 1972 by The Viking Press, Inc., 625 Madison Avenue, New York, N.Y. 10022. Published simultaneously in Canada by The Macmillan Company of Canada Limited. Library of Congress catalog card number: 70-183934. Printed in U.S.A. 821.08   1. Children's poetry
808.81   2. Nonsense verses
SBN 670-52107-8
1   2   3   4   5   76   75   74   73   72

Acknowledgment is made to the following for permission to use material owned by them. Every reasonable effort has been made to clear the use of the poems in this volume with the copyright owners. If notified of any omissions the editor and publisher will gladly make the proper corrections for future editions.

Angus and Robertson Ltd., for "Puddin' Song," reprinted from *The Magic Pudding,* by Norman Lindsay.

Delacorte Press, for "Yak," reprinted from *Mr. Smith and Other Nonsense* by William Jay Smith. Copyright © 1968 by William Jay Smith. A Seymour Lawrence Book/Delacorte Press. Used by permission of the publisher.

Dennis Dobson, London, for "Ant and Eleph-Ant," from *A Book of Milliganimals* by Spike Milligan; for "Down the Stream the Swans all Glide" and "Granny," from *Silly Verse for Kids* by Spike Milligan; for "Eels" and "Go North, South, East and West, Young Man," from *A Book of Bits or a Bit of a Book,* by Spike Milligan; and for "Questions, Quistions & Quoshtions," from *Little Pot Boiler* by Spike Milligan.

Dood, Mead & Company, and McClelland and Stewart Limited, for permission to reprint "The Bread-Knife Ballad," from *The Collected Poems of Robert Service.* Copyright 1940 by Robert Service. Copyright © renewed 1967.

Doubleday & Company, Inc., for "The Whale," copyright © 1961 by Theodore Roethke, "The Monotony Song," copyright © 1955 by Theodore Roethke from the book *The Collected Poems of Theodore Roethke.* Reprinted by permission of the publisher.

Harper & Row, Publishers, Inc., for "The Spangled Pandemonium," from *Beyond the Pawpaw Trees,* by Palmer Brown. Copyright 1954 by Palmer Brown. Reprinted by permission of the publishers.

J. B. Lippincott Company, for "The Witch! The Witch!" Copyright, 1926, renewal, 1954, by Eleanor Farjeon. From the book *Poems for Children,* Copyright 1951 by Eleanor Farjeon. Reprinted by permission of the publisher. Also from *Silver Sand & Snow,* by Eleanor Farjeon, reprinted by permission of Michael Joseph, Publishers, England.

Little, Brown and Company, for "The Poultries," reprinted from *Family Reunion,* by Ogden Nash. Copyright 1936 by The Curtis Publishing Company; for "The Dog," reprinted from *Everyone But Thee and Me,* by Ogden Nash. Copyright 1962 by Ogden Nash. Reprinted by permission of the publisher. Also for "The Unfortunate Grocer," reprinted from *Tirra Lirra,* by Laura E. Richards. Copyright 1932 by Laura E. Richards. Copyright 1955 by Little, Brown and Company; for "The Gingham Umbrella," reprinted from *Tirra Lirra,* by Laura E. Richards. Reprinted by permission of the publisher.

The Macmillian Company, for "The Hippopotamus," reprinted from *Toucans Two and Other Poems* by Jack Prelutsky. Copyright © 1967, 1970 by Jack Prelutsky. Reprinted with the permission of the publisher.

Curtis Brown Ltd., for "Howard," reprinted from *The Sunny Side,* by A. A. Milne.

G. P. Putnam's Sons, for "A Dreadful Sight," from *All Together,* by Dorothy Aldis. Copyright 1925, 1926, 1927, 1928, 1934, 1939, 1952 by Dorothy Aldis. Reprinted by permission of the publisher.

Alexander Resnikoff, for his poem, "Josephine,".

Routledge & Kegan Paul Ltd., and Dufour Editions, Inc., Chester Springs, Pennsylvania, for "King Arthur and His Knights," by Ruth Williams, reprinted from *Poems by Children,* edited by Michael Baldwin.

Charles Scribner's Sons, for "Song for Joey." Reprinted by permission of Charles Scribner's Sons from *The Wife of Winter,* by Michael Dennis Browne. Copyright © 1971 Michael Dennis Browne. "Hallelujah," by A. E. Housman is reprinted by permission of Charles Scribner's Sons from *My Brother, A. E. Housman,* by Laurence Housman. Copyright 1937, 1938 Laurence Housman; renewal copyright © 1965, 1966 Lloyds Bank Limited. Also by permission of The Society of Authors as the literary representative of the Estate of A. E. Housman, and Jonathan Cape Ltd., publishers of "A. E. H." by Laurence Housman.

Shel Silverstein, for his poems, "I Tried to Tip My Hat to Miss McCaffery," "The Generals," "If I Had a Brontosaurus," "Vegetables," "Rain," and "For Sale."

CONTENTS

INTRODUCTION

This book you hold,
Oh children dear,
Is nonsense verse—
But none by Lear,
None by Carroll,
None by Gilbert,
Who're all nutty
As a filbert.

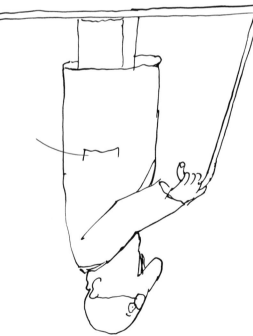

Why are none
Of these great wits
In this book?
I'll tell you, it's
Because, oh kids,
The chaps I've named
Are very, very,
Very famed;
And if you'll bother
For to look,
You'll find their stuff
In every book
Of nonsense verse
That's ever made;
And so their fame
Will never fade.

Their space, instead,
I will assign
To crazies like
Shel Silverstein
And to that prince
Of English silly men
The truly ludicrous
Spike Milligan
And many more
(To be meticulous)
Who help to sillify
OH, THAT'S RI*DIC*ULOUS!

WILLIAM COLE

Rain

I opened my eyes
And looked up at the rain
And it dripped in my head
And flowed into my brain
So pardon this wild crazy thing I just said
I'm just not the same since there's rain in my head.
I step very softly
I walk very slow
I can't do a hand-stand
Or I might overflow.
And all I can hear as I lie in my bed
Is the slishity-slosh of the rain in my head.

Shel Silverstein   *11*

Questions, Quistions & Quoshtions

Daddy how does an elephant feel
When he swallows a piece of steel?
Does he get drunk
And fall on his trunk
Or roll down the road like a wheel?

Daddy what would a pelican do
If he swallowed a bottle of glue?
Would his beak get stuck
Would he run out of luck
And lose his job at the zoo?

Son tell me tell me true,
If I belted you with a shoe,
Would you fall down dead?
Would you go up to bed?
—Either of those would do.

Spike Milligan

The Monot-
ony
Song

A donkey's tail is very nice
You mustn't pull it more than twice,
Now that's a piece of good advice
   —Heigho, meet Hugh and Harry!

One day Hugh walked up to a bear
And said, Old Boy, you're shedding hair,
And shedding more than here and there,
   —Heigho, we're Hugh and Harry!

The bear said, Sir, you go too far,
I wonder who you think you are
To make remarks about my—Grrrr!
   —And there was only Harry!

This Harry ran straight up a wall,
But found he wasn't there at all,
And so he had a horrid fall.
    —Alas, alack for Harry!

My sweetheart is a ugly witch,
And you should see her noses twitch,—
But Goodness Me, her father's rich!
    —And I'm not Hugh nor Harry!

This is, you see, a silly song
And you can sing it all day long—
You'll find I'm either right or wrong
    —Heigho Hugh and Harry!

The moral is, I guess you keep
Yourself awake until you sleep,
And sometimes look before you leap
    —Unless you're Hugh or Harry!

16   *Theodore Roethke*

King Arthur and his Knights,
Set out to fly their kites;
Because of too much breeze,
The kites caught on the trees.

Ruth Williams (age 13)

A Song
of Thanks

It's sensible that icicles
 Hang downward as they grow,
For I would hate to step on one
 That's buried in the snow.

It's really best that tides come in
　　And then return to sea;
For if they kept on coming in,
　　How wet we all would be!

I've often thought tomatoes are
　　Much better red than blue,
A blue tomato is a food
　　I'd certainly eschew.

It's best of all that everyone's
　　So tolerant today
That I can write this sort of stuff
　　And not get put away.

William Cole

Winkelman
Von Winkel

Winkelman Von Winkel is the wisest man alive,
He knows that one and one make two, and two and three make five;
He knows that water runs down hill, that the sun sets in the west,
And that for winter weather wear, one's winter clothes are best;
In fact, he does not mingle much with common folk around,
Because his learning is so great—his wisdom so profound.

Clara Odell Lyon

Three Hens

When three hens go a-walking, they
Observe this order and array:
The first hen walks in front, and then
Behind her walks the second hen,
While, move they slow or move they fast,
You find the third hen walking last.

Henry Johnstone

The Spangled Pandemonium

The spangled pandemonium
Is missing from the zoo.
He bent the bars the barest bit,
And slithered glibly through.

He crawled across the moated wall,
He climbed the mango tree,
And when the keeper scrambled up,
He nipped him in the knee.

To all of you, a warning
Not to wander after dark,
Or if you must, make very sure
You stay out of the park.

For the spangled pandemonium
Is missing from the zoo,
And since he nipped his keeper,
He would just as soon nip you!

Palmer Brown

For Sale

One sister for sale
One sister for sale
One crying and spying young sister for sale;
I'm really not kidding
So who'll start the bidding?
Do I hear a dollar?
A nickel?
A penny?
Isn't there, isn't there, isn't there any
One kid who will buy this old sister for sale?

Shel Silverstein

Ant
and Eleph-Ant

Said a tiny Ant
To the Elephant,
"Mind how you tread in this clearing!"

But alas! Cruel fate!
She was crushed by the weight
Of an Elephant, hard of hearing.

Spike Milligan

Yak

The long-haired Yak has long black hair,
He lets it grow—he doesn't care.
He lets it grow and grow and grow,
He lets it trail along the stair.
Does he ever go to the barbershop? NO!
How wild and woolly and devil-may-care
A long-haired Yak with long black hair
Would look when perched in a barber chair!

William Jay Smith

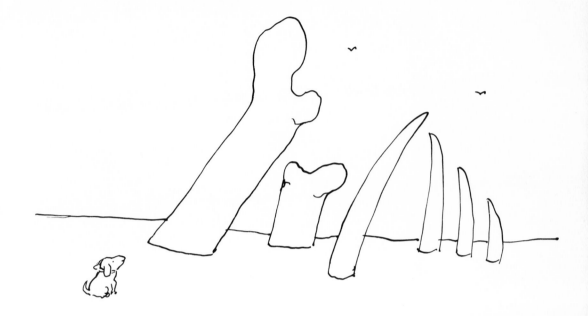

The Ichthyosaurus

There once was an Ichthyosaurus,
Who lived when the earth was all porous,
But he fainted with shame
When he first heard his name,
And departed a long time before us.

The
Ingenious
Little
Old Man

A little old man of the sea
Went out in a boat for a sail,
The water came in
Almost up to his chin
And he had nothing with which to bail.

But this little old man of the sea
Just drew out his jacknife so stout,
And a hole with its blade
In the bottom he made,
So that all of the water ran out.

John Bennett

Sneaky Bill

I'm Sneaky Bill, I'm terrible mean and vicious,
I steal all the cashews from the mixed-nuts dishes;
I eat all the icing but I won't touch the cake,
And what you won't give me, I'll go ahead and take.
I gobble up the cherries from everyone's drinks,
And if there's sausages I grab a dozen links;
I take both drumsticks if there's turkey or chicken,
And the biggest strawberries are what I'm pickin';
I make sure I get the finest chop on the plate,
And I'll eat the portions of anyone who's late!

I'm always on the spot before the dinner bell—
I guess I'm pretty awful,
                      but
                         I
                            do
                                eat
                                    well!

William Cole

Josephine

Josephine, Josephine,
The meanest girl I've ever seen.
Her eyes are red, her hair is green
And she takes baths in gasoline.

Alexander Resnikoff 31

Twins

Here's a baby! Here's another!
A sister and her infant brother.
Which is which is hard to tell—
But mother knows them very well.

Lucy Fitch Perkins

The Witch!

The witch! The witch! Don't let her get you!
Or your Aunt wouldn't know you the next time she met you!

Eleanor Farjeon

A Dreadful Sight

We saw him so naughty and scratching and hitting
And when he sat down, then he wouldn't stop sitting,
Right on the sidewalk with everyone staring,
But he didn't care—oh, he LIKED it not caring!

Dorothy Aldis

34

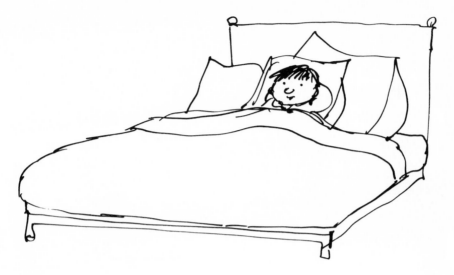

Go North,
South,
East and West,
Young Man

Drake is going West, lads,
So Tom is going East;
But tiny Fred
Just lies in bed,
The lazy little beast.

Spike Milligan

Vegetables

Eat a tomato and you'll turn red
(I don't think that's really so);
Eat a carrot and you'll turn orange
(Still and all you never know);
Eat some spinach and you'll turn green
(I'm not saying that it's true
But that's what I heard, and so
I thought I'd pass it on to you).

Shel Silverstein

Daisy Deborah Delilah Dean

Daisy Deborah Delilah Dean,
Fresh as a rose and proud as a queen!
Daisy Deborah, drawn from the pool
By Harry and Dick, came dripping to school.
Daisy Deborah, wet as a fish,
Her mother says *bed*
Her father says *pish!*

Children's rhyme

The Roof

The roof it has a lazy time,
    A-lying in the sun;
The walls, they have to hold him up;
    They do not have much fun!

Gelett Burgess

Eels

Eileen Carroll
Had a barrel
Filled with writhing eels
And just for fun
She swallowed one:
Now she knows how it feels.

Spike Milligan

The
Unfortunate Grocer

There was a good grocer
Who never said, "No sir!"
  When dainties his customers sought.
Whatever their asking,
His brain he'd be tasking,
  To buy anything could be bought.

Elephant's ear and tapir's tongue,
Pelican's pouch ("Be sure it's young!")
Saddle of yak ("How long has it hung?")
  Ostrich's eggs ("New-laid!")
Buffalo milk ("Fermented!") to quaff,
Laughing jackass ("We want the laugh!")
And "Can't you get me a sucking giraffe?
  You've always been amply paid!"

The unfortunate grocer
(Who never said, "No sir!")
    On hearing this, took to his bed.
"'Tis hopeless to please them,
I never can ease them,
    I'd better be dying!" he said.

Laura E. Richards

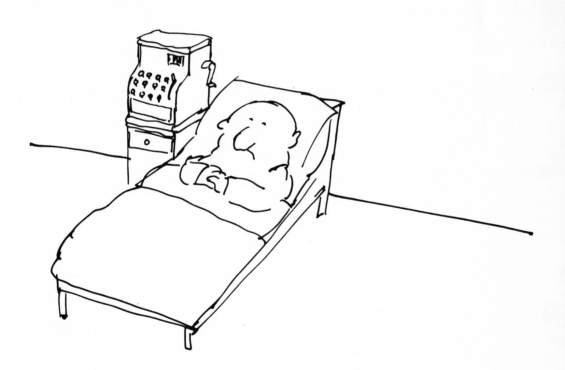

Godfrey Gordon Gustavus Gore

Godfrey Gordon Gustavus Gore—
No doubt you have heard the name before—
Was a boy who never would shut a door!

The wind might whistle, the wind might roar,
And teeth be aching and throats be sore,
But still he never would shut the door.

His father would beg, his mother implore,
"Godfrey Gordon Gustavus Gore,
We really *do* wish you would shut the door!"

Their hands they wrung, their hair they tore;
But Godfrey Gordon Gustavus Gore
Was deaf as the buoy out at the Nore.

When he walked forth the folks would roar,
"Godfrey Gordon Gustavus Gore
Why don't you think to shut the door?"

They rigged out a Shutter with sail and oar,
And threatened to pack off Gustavus Gore
On a voyage of penance to Singapore.

But he begged for mercy, and said, "No more!
Pray do not send me to Singapore
On a Shutter, and then I will shut the door!"

"You will?" said his parents; "then keep on shore!
But mind you do! For the plague is sore
Of a fellow that never will shut the door,
Godfrey Gordon Gustavus Gore!"

William Brighty Rands

If I Had
a Brontosaurus

If I had a brontosaurus
I would name him Morris or Horace;
But if suddenly one day he had a lot of little brontosauri
I would change his name to Laurie.

Shel Silverstein

The
Cassowary

Once there was a cassowary
On the plains of Timbuctoo
Killed and ate a missionary
Skin and bones and hymn-book too.

English children's rhyme

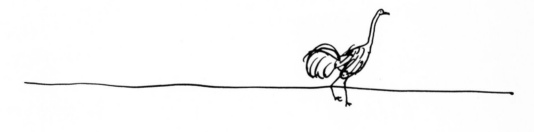

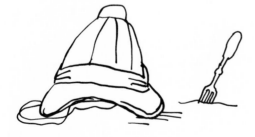

Song for Joey

O I can sell you a talking plum
I can sell you a squeaking rose
I can hire you a horse as thin as your thumb
But you'll have to pay through the nose the nose
O you'll have to pay through the nose

O I can give you a grinning fish
I can give you an apple that snows
I can find you a king who is fit for a dish
But you'll have to pay through the nose the nose
O you'll have to pay through the nose

O floating foxes O squirrels that sneeze
O world that nobody knows
O I can give you whatever you please
But you'll have to pay through the nose the nose
O you'll have to pay through the nose

Michael Dennis Browne   47

A Surprise

When the donkey saw the zebra
  He began to switch his tail;
"Well, I never!" was his comment—
  "Here's a mule that's been to jail!"

Malcolm Douglas

That Head

I suppose I've passed
   him a hundred times,
    but I always stop
     for a minute
And look at his head,
   that tragic head,
    the head
      with nobody in it.

Jerce Bullmer

The Generals

Said General Clay to General Gore,
"Oh *must* we fight this silly war,

To kill and die is such a bore."
"I quite agree," said General Gore.

Said General Gore to General Clay,
"We *could* go to the beach today
And have some ice cream on the way."
"A *grand* idea," said General Clay.

Said General Clay to General Gore,
"We'll build sand castles on the shore."
Said General Gore, "We'll splash and play."
"Let's go *right now*," said General Clay.

Said General Gore to General Clay,
"But what if the sea is *closed* today?
And what if the sand's been blown away?"
"A *dreadful* thought," said General Clay.

Said General Gore to General Clay,
"I've always feared the ocean's spray
And we may drown—it's true, we may,
And we may even drown today."
"Too true, too true," said General Clay.

Said General Clay to General Gore,
"My bathing suit is slightly tore,
We'd better go on with our war."
"I quite agree," said General Gore.

Then General Clay charged General Gore
As bullets flew and cannon roared.
And now, alas! there is no more
Of General Clay and General Gore.

Shel Silverstein

I've got a dog as thin as a rail,
He's got fleas all over his tail;
Every time his tail goes flop,
The fleas on the bottom all hop to the top.

Anonymous

54

The Poultries

Let's think of eggs.
They have no legs.
Chickens come from eggs,
But they have legs.
The plot thickens;
Eggs come from chickens,
But have no legs under 'em.
What a conundrum!

Ogden Nash

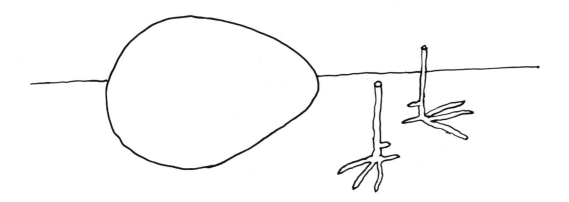

Uncle

Uncle, whose inventive brains
Kept evolving aeroplanes,
Fell from an enormous height
On my garden lawn, last night.
  Flying is a fatal sport,
  Uncle wrecked the tennis court.

Harry Graham

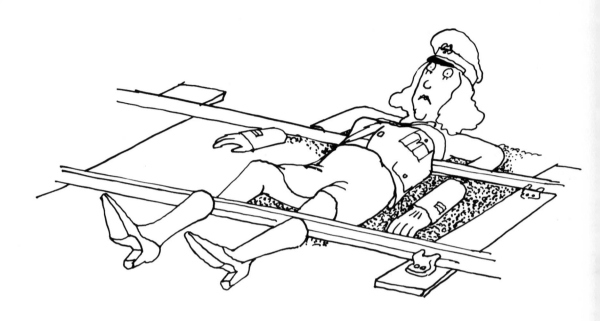

Hallelujah!

"Hallelujah!" was the only observation
That escaped Lieutenant-Colonel Mary Jane,
When she tumbled off the platform in the station,
And was cut in little pieces by the train.
    Mary Jane, the train is through yer!
    Hallelujah, Hallelujah!
We shall gather up the fragments that remain.

A. E. Housman   *57*

Story of Reginald

Cousin Reg is a charming boy—
Just like little Lord Fauntleroy.
All day long he sweetly prattles
Of animals, fairies, kings, and battles.

Dear little chap . . . he bores me stiff!
We'll go for a walk to the top of the cliff;
The cliff is steep and it's lonely, too—
What an adventure, Reg, for you.

Cousin Reg was a charming boy,
Just like little Lord Fauntleroy. . . .

Hubert Phillips

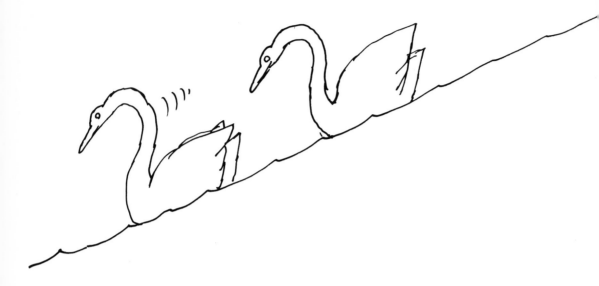

Down the Stream the Swans All Glide

Down the stream the swans all glide;
It's quite the cheapest way to ride.
Their legs get wet,
Their tummies wetter:
I think after all
The bus is better.

Spike Milligan

Howard

There was a young puppy called Howard,
Who at fighting was rather a coward;
   He never quite ran
   When the battle began,
But he started at once to bow-wow hard.

A. A. Milne

A Young Lady of Spain

There was a young lady of Spain
Who was dreadfully sick on a train,
  Not once, but again
  And again and again,
And again and again and again.

Anonymous

The Whale

There was a most Monstrous Whale:
He had no Skin, he had no Tail.
When he tried to Spout, that Great Big Lubber,
The best he could do was Jiggle his Blubber.

Theodore Roethke

What a Beautiful Word!

Ah, swallow . . . swallow—what a beautiful word!
(No, no, not the gulp! I mean the bird!)

William Cole

Unselfishness

All those who see my children say,
   "What sweet, what kind, what charming elves!"
They are so thoughtful, too, for they
   Are *always* thinking of themselves.
It must be ages since I ceased
To wonder which I liked the least.

Such is their generosity,
   That, when the roof began to fall,
They would not share the risk with me,
   But said, "No, father, take it all!"
Yet I should love them more, I know,
If I did not dislike them so.

Harry Graham

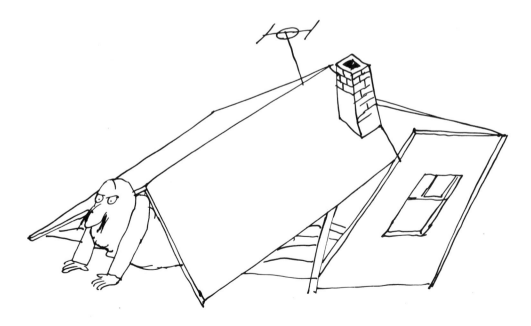

The Gingham Umbrella

(A LESSON IN POLITENESS)

Alphonso, Alphonso, Alphonso and Arabella,
   They happened to meet
   A man in the street,
Who carried a gingham umbrella.

Alphonso possessed neither manners nor grace,
He made at this person a hideous face;
But how different the conduct of sweet Arabella,
Who praised with politeness the gingham umbrella.

The man was a nobleman, deeply disguised;
The compliment courteous he pointedly prized;
"Sweet creature," he said, "come away from this feller,
And take both my heart and my gingham umbrella!"

The very next morning they met in the church,
And foolish Alphonso was left in the lurch;
For they said, "In the future you'll know how to tell a
Great lord from a loon, by his gingham umbrella!"

Laura E. Richards   67

The Dog

The truth I do not stretch or shove
When I state the dog is full of love.
I've also proved, by actual test,
A wet dog is the lovingest.

Ogden Nash

Remarkable truly, is art!
See—elliptical wheels on a cart!
It looks very fair
In the picture up there;
But imagine the ride when you start!

Gelett Burgess

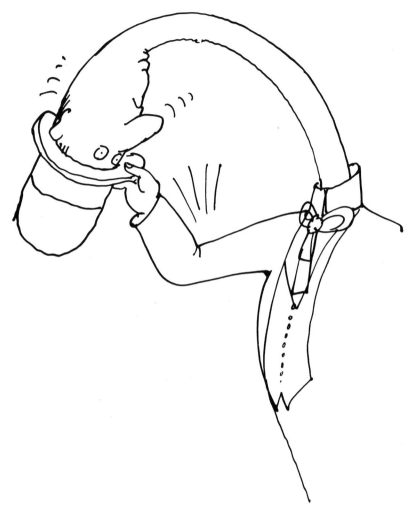

I tried to tip my hat to Miss McCaffery,
But I guess I must have had it on too tight,
'Cause it wouldn't come off my head,
And my neck got stretched instead.
And that's what you get for tryin' to be polite.

Shel Silverstein

Granny

Through every nook and every cranny
The wind blew in on poor old Granny;
Around her knees, into each ear
(And up her nose as well, I fear).

All through the night the wind grew worse,
It nearly made the vicar curse.
The top had fallen off the steeple
Just missing him (and other people).

It blew on man; it blew on beast.
It blew on nun; it blew on priest.
It blew the wig off Auntie Fanny—
But most of all, it blew on Granny! !

Spike Milligan   71

The Bread-Knife Ballad

I

A little child was sitting
Upon her mother's knee,
And down her cheeks the bitter tears did flow;
And as I sadly listened
I heard this tender plea;
'Twas uttered in a voice so soft and low:—

Chorus:

Please, Mother, don't stab Father with the bread-knife.
Remember 'twas a gift when you were wed.
But if you *must* stab Father with the bread-knife,
Please, Mother, use another for the bread.

II

"Not guilty!" said the Jury,
And the Judge said: "Set her free;
But remember, it must not occur again;
And next time you must listen
To your little daughter's plea,"
Then all the Court did join in this refrain:—

Chorus . . .

Robert Service   *73*

Puddin' Song

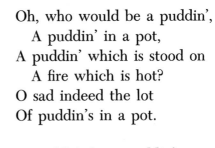

Oh, who would be a puddin',
  A puddin' in a pot,
A puddin' which is stood on
  A fire which is hot?
O sad indeed the lot
Of puddin's in a pot.

I wouldn't be a puddin'
  If I could be a bird,
If I could be a wooden
  Doll, I would'n' say a word.
Yes, I have often heard
It's grand to be a bird.

But as I am a puddin',
  A puddin' in a pot,
I hope you get the stomachache
  For eatin' me a lot.
I hope you get it hot,
You puddin'-eatin' lot!

Norman Lindsay

The Hippopotamus

The huge hippopotamus hasn't a hair
on the back of his wrinkly hide;
he carries the bulk of his prominent hulk
rather loosely assembled inside.

The huge hippopotamus lives without care
at a slow philosophical pace,
as he wades in the mud with a thump and a thud
and a permanent grin on his face.

Jack Prelutsky   75

A Norrible Tale

A norrible tale I'm going to tell
Of the woful tragedy which befell
A family that once resided
In the very same thorofare as I did;

Indeed it is a norrible tale,
'Twill make your faces all turn pale,
And your cheeks with tears will be overcome,
Tweedle twaddle, tweedle twaddle twum.

The father in the garden went to walk,
And he cut his throat with a piece of chalk;
The mother, at this was so cut-up
She drowned herself in the water-butt.

The eldest sister, on bended knees
Strangled herself with toasted cheese;
The eldest brother, a charming fella,
Blew out his brains with a gingham umbrella.

The innocent infant lying in the cradle,
Shot itself dead with a silver ladle;
And the maid-servant, not knowing what she did,
Strangled herself with the saucepan lid.

The cat sitting down by the kitchen fire,
Chewed up the fender and did expire;
And a fly on the ceiling—this case is the worst 'un—
Blew itself up with spontaneous combustion.

Now this here family of which I've sung,
If they had not died should have all been hung;
For had they ne'er done themselves any wrong
Why, they might have been here to have heard this song.

Old English music hall song

AUTHOR INDEX

TITLE INDEX

J
821.08
C   Cole
              Oh, that's ridiculous!

APR 3 0 73	414	OCT 27 '82 7704
JUN 14 73	436	7 APR 1 6453
JUN 29 '73	Renewal	MAY 9 '89
APR 8 74	3766	MAY 02 2000 4834